JIM
BRIDGER

TRAPPER, TRADER, AND GUIDE

SPECIAL LIVES IN HISTORY THAT BECOME

Signature LIVES

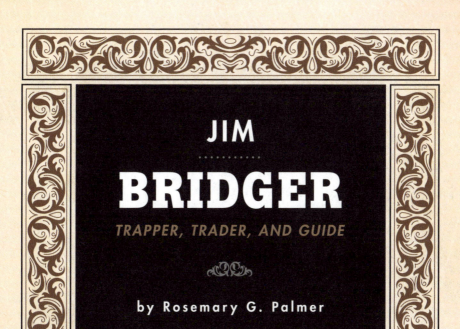

JIM
BRIDGER
TRAPPER, TRADER, AND GUIDE

by Rosemary G. Palmer

Content Adviser: Fred R. Gowans,
Professor of History Emeritus
Brigham Young University

Reading Adviser: Katie Van Sluys, Ph.D.,
School of Education, DePaul University

COMPASS POINT BOOKS MINNEAPOLIS, MINNESOTA

Compass Point Books
3109 West 50th Street, #115
Minneapolis, MN 55410

Visit Compass Point Books on the Internet at *www.compasspointbooks.com*
or e-mail your request to *custserv@compasspointbooks.com*

Editor: Sue Vander Hook
Page Production: Noumenon Creative
Photo Researcher: Lori Bye
Cartographer: XNR Productions, Inc.
Library Consultant: Kathleen Baxter

Art Director: Jaime Martens
Creative Director: Keith Griffin
Editorial Director: Carol Jones
Managing Editor: Catherine Neitge

Library of Congress Cataloging-in-Publication Data
Palmer, Rosemary G.
  Jim Bridger: trapper, trader, and guide / by Rosemary G. Palmer.
    p. cm.—(Signature lives)
  Includes bibliographical references and index.
  ISBN-13: 978-0-7565-1870-7 (hardcover)
  ISBN-10: 0-7565-1870-9 (hardcover)
  ISBN-13: 978-0-7565-1975-9 (paperback)
  ISBN-10: 0-7565-1975-6 (paperback)
  1. Bridger, Jim, 1804–1881—Juvenile literature. 2. Pioneers—West
(U.S.)—Biography—Juvenile literature. 3. Scouts and scouting—West
(U.S.)—Biography—Juvenile literature. 4. Trappers—West (U.S.)—
Biography—Juvenile literature. 5. West (U.S.)—Biography—Juvenile
literature. I. Title. II. Series.
  F592.B85P35 2007
  978'.02092—dc22   2006002998

AMERICAN FRONTIER ERA

The young United States was growing at a rapid pace. Settlers were pushing west, conquering and building from coast to coast. World leaders hammered out historic agreements, such as the Louisiana Purchase in 1803, which drastically increased U.S. territory. This westward movement often led to bitter conflicts with Native Americans trying to protect their way of life and their traditional lands. Life on the frontier was often filled with danger and difficulties. The people who wove their way into American history overcame these challenges with a courage and conviction that defined an era and shaped a nation.

Table of Contents

1 TENSION ON THE TRAIL

❦

The last Sunday of June 1862 was pleasant and peaceful. Two federal judges and their families were moving West to the Utah Territory. A military company was taking them there, and Jim Bridger was their guide.

The group set up camp near the Sweetwater River, which provided drinking water for the parched travelers. Some of the men cleaned their guns and equipment, and others tramped into the hills to hunt.

Late that afternoon, the men collected sagebrush to start their campfires and cook supper. Suddenly, a stranger rode into their camp and shouted, "Indians! Indians!" He jumped off his horse and approached the commanding officer. His wagon train, which was

As people moved West in the 1800s, Indians sometimes reacted violently when white men invaded and took over their land.

Jim Bridger
(1804–1881)

just 5 miles (8 kilometers) behind them, had been attacked. Their wagons had been rolling along in single file, but the last wagon trailed far behind the others. An Indian war party had attacked the lone wagon at the back, killed two men, and stole their horses.

Immediately, the commanding officer of Bridger's group ordered Bridger and 20 other men to rush to the scene. William Brackett, one of the men who went with Bridger, later said:

> After a hard gallop of some five miles we came up with the emigrants in camp. Their wagons were parked in a circle with their horses and fires inside, and armed men marched about on guard.

Brackett and Bridger rode their horses over a hill and spotted the covered wagon that had been attacked. Some distance from the wagon they found the body of an older man. Brackett later wrote about the grisly scene:

Bridger calmly dismounted, knelt on the ground and closely examined the foot prints around the body. Then he pulled three arrows from the old man's corpse and closely examined them. "Arapahoes and Cheyennes," he said, as he followed the blood creases on the arrows with critical eyes.

Walking over to the wagon, Bridger observed pieces of harness scattered around the ground. The Indians must have taken the horses after cutting their harnesses with knives. The body of a young man still clutching his revolver lay next to the wagon. Brackett wrote:

As soon as Bridger saw the pistol he walked around the wagon in a circle, carefully examining the grass and sage brush. Suddenly he stooped and seized a piece of sage brush and broke it off. On it was a speck of blood. Widening his search he soon found more blood and came back saying: "The boy has peppered one of the scamps, anyway!"

Bridger and Brackett wrapped

The Sweetwater River, a branch of the North Platte River, is approximately 150 miles (241 km) long and flows through central Wyoming. From present-day Casper, Wyoming, wagon trains heading West would follow the Sweetwater through central Wyoming to the Continental Divide. Travelers often stopped by the Sweetwater to carve their names on Independence Rock and visit Devil's Gate, which was a few miles southwest of the rock.

A wagon train made its way west along the Sweetwater River and past Independence Rock on the Oregon Trail.

the bodies in blankets, and members of the wagon train buried them alongside the trail. After failing to find the attackers, Bridger returned to his government wagon train and took the travelers on to Salt Lake City, Utah.

With Bridger's vast knowledge of the American West, other wagon companies crossing the Plains would hire him as their trusted guide. He would live in the West for more than 30 years and come to know the layout of the land as though he had a map in his head.

Although Jim Bridger never received a formal education or learned to read and write, he had other valuable abilities. He excelled in wilderness skills and could find the best routes through uncharted Western territory. He would become one of the most famous mountain men, trappers, hunters, trailblazers, Army scouts, and guides of 19th-century America. ❧

2 CHILDHOOD YEARS

Chapter

⌯⌲⌯

James "Jim" Bridger was born on March 17, 1804, in Richmond, Virginia. He was the first child of James and Chloe Bridger. The United States was still a new nation when Jim was born. The American Revolution had ended officially just 21 years before, in 1783, and now the country wanted to expand and grow. President Thomas Jefferson was curious to learn about the vast territory west of the Mississippi River.

In 1803, a year before Jim's birth, Jefferson purchased 827,987 square miles (2.2 million sq km) of territory from France. It stretched from the Mississippi River to the Rocky Mountains. The Louisiana Purchase, as it was called, doubled the size of the United States. Jefferson appointed a group of Army

Boats carried people and goods along the Mississippi River on their way to busy ports like St. Louis, Missouri.

*Meriwether
Lewis
(1774–1809)*

*William Clark
(1770–1838)*

officers to explore the land. Meriwether Lewis and William Clark were chosen to lead the expedition. Several weeks after Jim was born, Lewis and Clark's group set out to explore the West. Little did Jim's parents know that their son would one day go to the same region to explore, trap, and trade.

Jim's father was a farmer, land surveyor, and tavern owner. His mother managed the tavern, a type of inn for travelers. The Bridger family was growing, and a daughter and another son soon joined the family. However, very little is known about Jim's family or early life. We do know that in 1812, Jim's father learned about cheap, fertile land near the Mississippi River. He purchased a covered wagon and loaded his family and possessions inside. Jim was 8 years old when his parents made the trip by wagon to Six Mile Prairie, Illinois, just across the river from St. Louis, Missouri. Other settlers were also coming to this area of rich vegetation and fertile soil.

With his surveying skills, Jim's father found work in the new region. Often his assignments took him away from home. As the oldest child, Jim was given plenty of responsibility. His younger sister and brother also pitched in with simple tasks around the house and farm.

Near Six Mile Prairie flowed the mighty Mississippi River. Boys often fished its waters and carried their catch home for supper. They watched as passengers, wagons, farm goods, and animals were carried on a ferryboat back and forth across the river to St. Louis.

The year before Jim Bridger was born, the United States purchased the Louisiana Territory from France. Other nations still controlled vast areas of North America.

St. Louis grew rapidly as a trade center and a central shipping port.

As Jim watched the rugged men who operated the boats and rafts, he became familiar with the river's wonders and dangers.

Four years after the Bridgers moved to Six Mile Prairie, Jim's mother died. As the story goes, Jim's aunt came from Virginia to help take care of the children. But there were more tragedies to come. That same year, Jim's little brother died, and the next year, in 1817, his father died.

Now 13-year-old Jim and his sister were orphans. No one knows for sure what happened to Jim's sister, but Jim began operating a ferry between Six Mile Prairie and St. Louis. Later, he found work in St. Louis as an apprentice to a blacksmith named Phil Creamer. As he pounded and shaped the hot iron on an anvil with a heavy sledge, Jim grew strong. He worked hard to learn the blacksmith trade.

St. Louis was growing into a prosperous fur-trading center. Traders floated buffalo hides and furs from beaver, bear, fox, and other animals on boats down the Mississippi River. They sold and traded most of their furs in St. Louis and then set out again to hunt and trap in the wilderness. While they were in the city, they stocked up on supplies.

As St. Louis continued to grow and prosper, the city welcomed the first steamboat in 1817. People cheered as it docked at the foot of Market Street. This new invention made the town an even busier place. Jewelers, bricklayers, cabinetmakers, and bakers arrived. Doctors and lawyers came, and newspapers reported current

St. Louis became part of the United States with the Louisiana Purchase. From 1812 to 1821, the town served as the capital of Missouri Territory. After Missouri became a state, Jefferson City replaced St. Louis as the state capital.

St. Louis grew to be one of the greatest river ports in the United States. During the mid-1800s, it was the "Gateway to the West" for people moving to the Pacific Coast and western lands.

As a blacksmith, Bridger learned to shape horseshoes and other metal objects on the hot forge.

events. Within two years, steamboats became a common sight in this Mississippi River town.

By 1820, St. Louis had 4,500 residents and 300 new buildings. People bought and sold produce at the market house in the public square. Yapping dogs, snorting pigs, and cattle roamed streets that were either muddy or dusty, depending on the weather. While some children attended school at home, many received little or no education. Jim was one who never learned to read or write. He was too busy working.

Spending his days in Creamer's blacksmith shop opened up the world for Jim. Adventurers strolled in needing horseshoes and guns. They had wagons that needed to be repaired and many stories to share. Sixteen-year-old Jim knew the heat of the forge, the whooshing of the bellows, and the ring of the anvil. He watched the hot iron sizzle as he shoved it into a barrel of cold water.

As he developed his blacksmithing skills, Jim heard people tell tales about the fur trade and places he could only imagine. About two weeks before Jim turned 18, an ad appeared in the newspaper. It would change his life forever. ❧

3 TRADER AND TRAPPER

ecxƆ

On March 6, 1822, Andrew Henry and William Henry Ashley, partners in a Missouri lead-mining business, placed an advertisement in the *Missouri Republican* newspaper:

> *To Enterprising Young Men*
> *The subscriber wishes to engage ONE HUNDRED MEN to ascend the river Missouri to its sources, there to be employed, for one, two, or three years. For particulars, enquire of Major Andrew Henry, near the Lead Mines, in the County of Washington (who will ascend with, and command the party) or to the subscriber at St. Louis.*

Henry and Ashley wanted men who would barter

for animal furs trapped by Indians. Beaver pelts especially were in high demand because beaver top hats were the latest men's fashion in Europe. Each man would be paid $200 to $400 a year, a good salary for that time. The *St. Louis Enquirer* reported that the group was made up of "young men, many of whom have relinquished the most respectable employments and circles of society, for this ... undertaking." They were called Ashley's Hundred or the Henry-Ashley party.

Jedediah Smith (1798–1831) was a fur trapper and explorer of the American frontier.

Without a family or home of his own, Bridger didn't have a problem leaving St. Louis. He joined the expedition. Some of the other young men who signed up were Jedediah Smith, Jim Beckwourth, Hugh Glass, James Clyman, and William Sublette. They all would become well-known for their roles in developing the American West.

Near the end of March, two large keelboats rocked in the water of the St. Louis wharf. Each boat was equipped with a sail, poles, and towropes. If there wasn't enough wind for sailing, boatmen would push poles against the river bottom and send the boat upstream against the current. When the water was too swift for poles, 12 to 15 horsemen along the bank would pull the boat along with tow-ropes. This was slow, difficult work.

Early in April, one of the keelboats left St. Louis with one group of the Henry-Ashley party onboard. Jim Bridger was among them, and Andrew Henry was their leader. The adventurers headed up the Missouri River on their way to the mouth of the Yellowstone River in present-day North Dakota. Covering 8 to 12 miles (13 to 19 km) a day, they stopped to shoot squirrels, turkeys, and occasionally a deer or buffalo for food. They also caught catfish in the river.

Two weeks later, the second keelboat left from St. Louis. Onboard were the rest of the men along with supplies they would need for trading. About 100 miles (160 km) upriver, however, this boat capsized, and the boatman returned to St. Louis to

James Beckwourth (c. 1800–1866) was an experienced scout and mountain man during America's westward expansion.

get a new boat.

In the meantime, Henry's men built a trading post at the mouth of the Yellowstone River. They named it Fort Henry. When Ashley's supply boat finally reached the fort, it was too late in the season to barter for furs. The Indians had already sold their pelts. Ashley returned to St. Louis to purchase more supplies for the next spring, and Henry remained at the fort with the men.

During the winter of 1822–1823, Bridger learned how to trade for furs and how to survive in the wilderness. Henry divided his men into two teams—one would trade with the Crow Indian tribe and the other with the Blackfeet. Bridger was probably

A trapper crossing a mountain stream

part of Captain John Weber's party who set out to find the Crows.

Both teams were unsuccessful, however, and returned to Fort Henry with nothing to show for their work. Henry sent Jedediah Smith down the Missouri River to find Ashley and ask him to bring more horses. Ashley bought some horses at an Arikara Indian village. But when trouble broke out, the Indians stole the horses and attacked Ashley's group, killing 12 and wounding 11.

Those left in Ashley's party fled downstream. Ashley sent letters to Henry at the fort and to the Army in St. Louis asking them to punish the Arikaras. Bridger was part of Henry's group that joined forces with Ashley and burned the Arikara villages. Although the Indians rebuilt their homes, they never forgave these white Americans for what they did.

The upper Missouri River area where the Arikaras lived was now unsafe for trading. Henry and Ashley decided to barter in another region with the Crows. The entrepreneurs were desperate to keep their business alive. They couldn't make money unless

> *John H. Weber (1779–1859) was born in Europe, moved to Missouri, and at the age of 43 joined the Henry-Ashley expedition in 1822. Jim Bridger was often in Weber's brigade. Weber trapped in what is now south-western Wyoming and northern Utah. Weber County and the Weber River in present-day Utah were named after him. By 1827, Weber left the trapper's life and returned to the Midwest.*

they had furs to take back to St. Louis.

Meanwhile, Ashley returned to Missouri for more supplies, and Henry again organized his men into two teams. One group led by Smith set out in search of the Crow tribe. Henry led Bridger and other traders back to Fort Henry to close it down and pick up the supplies and the men who were guarding the fort. On the way, Hugh Glass wandered off from the group. Fellow trader James Clyman wrote about what happened:

James Clyman (1792–1881)

Amongst this party was a Mr Hugh Glass who could not be rstrand [restrained] ... he went off of the line of march one afternoon and met with a large grissly Bear which he shot at and wounded   the bear as is usual attacted Glass   he attemptd to climb a tree but the bear caught him and hauled [him] to the ground tearing and lacerating his body in feareful rate.

By now, several of Henry's men were in gunshot

range of the bear. They fired their guns, and the bear fell dead on Glass' body. Henry asked two of his men to stay with their badly injured partner. After five days and nights, the men decided Glass wouldn't survive. They also worried that the Arikaras might attack. So they left the dying man alone and rushed

Bears sometimes were a threat to explorers in the West.

back to Fort Henry. To their surprise, Glass lived and slowly made his way to Fort Kiowa on the Missouri River. Although Glass never identified the two traders who abandoned him, Bridger most likely was one of them.

After Henry's men closed down Fort Henry, they took their trading supplies to the mouth of the Big Horn River in present-day Montana. Bridger spent the winter of 1823–1824 there. He kept in contact with Smith's group, who had found the Crow Indians in the Wind River Valley of present-day Wyoming.

The Crows gave Smith's group useful information. They told the men about a pass at the south end of the Wind River Mountains that led to the Green River, where beaver were plentiful. In March 1824, Smith led his men across what came to be called South Pass. By midsummer, both of the Henry-Ashley teams had crossed the pass. Bridger and his fellow traders were now in the territory where the Shoshone and Ute Indians lived. But these Indians didn't trap beaver. The Henry-Ashley party would have to find

South Pass is on the Continental Divide in Wyoming. Not a treacherous mountain pass, it is a 20-mile (32-km) gap at the southern end of the Wind River Mountains. One emigrant wrote, "The ascent is so gradual, that one scarcely knows when one is at the summit." In 1811, a party of fur trappers led by Robert Stuart crossed South Pass. Jedediah Smith's company rediscovered South Pass in 1824 and prepared the way for covered wagon pioneers.

and trap their own.

From the Crows and other Indians who knew the land so well, Bridger learned about streams, mountains, and landmarks. He developed a homing instinct that helped him always find his way back to camp. This made him an excellent mountain man, guide, and trustworthy scout. Whatever the trail or the weather, Bridger could find his way. He understood the layout of the land and used all five of his senses to get around.

Bridger also learned how to trap beaver in the fall and spring. The best pelts came in the spring when beavers had winter-thick fur. Trapping was hard work, even for a young man like Bridger, whose

Although some westward travelers were afraid of the Indians, others befriended them and learned from them about the land.

muscles had been strengthened by using a forge and anvil. After scouting for signs of beaver, Bridger waded into icy waters at dusk to place his traps. In the morning, he often found beavers in the traps. He removed the hides and took them to camp, where he scraped and stretched them.

During the fall of 1824, Bridger and Weber's group had great success trapping beavers. Sometimes they caught them on the Bear River in present-day southwestern Wyoming. At the Utah-Idaho border, one trapper wrote that they approached "a small sweet lake, about 120 miles [192 km] in circumference, with beautiful, clear water, and when the wind blows has a splendid appearance." He was describing Bear Lake. The men would return there two more times to go to a fur-trading event that came to be called a rendezvous.

The trappers moved on to Willow Valley in the Wasatch Mountains near present-day Logan, Utah. Willows grew abundantly along numerous streams in this valley that was "surrounded by stupendous mountains, which are unrivalled for beauty and serenity of scenery." Weber's men trapped beaver there in the Logan, Blacksmith's Fork, and Bear rivers. Then they cached, or hid, their furs in caves they dug in the soil or riverbank until they were ready to trade them. As a result, they changed the name of the place to Cache Valley.

When the streams froze over in the winter of 1824–1825, Weber's men settled in at present-day Cove Creek in Cache Valley. This was the first winter quarters for these traders who came to be known as mountain men. During the winter months, Bridger and the other men learned about trapping, hunting, exploring, and repairing equipment. They coped with blizzards and deep snow and engaged in what was called busy idleness. By the campfire, Bridger sometimes sewed his own clothes, played cards, told tales, and sang songs. Some of the men read—if they knew how.

Mountain men often scouted the countryside alone with just their packhorses and supplies. They were looking for the best places to trap for furs.

As spring arrived in 1825, Bridger and other curious members of the group began wondering where the present-day Bear River flowed south from Cache Valley. They chose 21-year-old Bridger to find out. Bridger's quiet manner and good judgment often earned him additional responsibilities and assignments. He would need a boat, so he stretched buffalo hides over a willow frame and made what was called a bull boat. It was a simple boat that would take him down the Bear River.

Bridger traveled down the river until it emptied into a huge body of water. He climbed out of his boat, walked along the shore, and tasted the water. To his surprise, it was very salty. He rushed back to tell the others that he had discovered part of the Pacific Ocean. It was actually a huge salty lake that came to be called the Great Salt Lake. Although many thought Bridger was the first white man to see the lake, trapper Etienne Provost from Taos had already viewed it in the fall of 1824.

While Bridger was exploring the Great Salt Lake, Ashley was preparing to bring supplies by pack animals to the mountains. Now that his fur traders were also excellent

The Great Salt Lake is three to five times saltier than the ocean. A remnant of ancient Lake Bonneville, it covers around 1,700 square miles (4,420 sq km). The Bear, Weber, and Jordan rivers feed into the Great Salt Lake, but it has no outlet to the sea. Because of its high salt content, only tiny brine shrimp, bacteria, and algae live in its waters.

trappers, Ashley saw a new way to do business. Instead of making his fur traders haul furs to St. Louis, the men would stay in the mountains all year and do their own trapping. Horse and mule pack trains would bring supplies to a designated place, pick the furs up there, and then take them back to Missouri. In July 1825, Bridger and his fellow trappers met Ashley's supply train in southwestern Wyoming. They exchanged supplies and furs at the first mountain man rendezvous—an event at which the men would meet every year. ૭ঌ

The Great Salt Lake is located northwest of present-day Salt Lake City, Utah.

4 MOUNTAIN MAN RENDEZVOUS

ೲೲ

The 1825 mountain man rendezvous was a special event. Bridger and his fellow trappers had gathered up their furs in Cache Valley and headed to southwest Wyoming. Ashley's supply caravan had also arrived. There were about 150 men who attended. At this one-day gathering, white and Indian traders exchanged pelts for goods they would need for the coming year. Two dozen Iroquois Indians brought furs to trade. They were now hunting and trapping with the white Americans.

At the end of the day, Ashley packed up the furs he had received in trade and hauled them to the Big Horn River. Then he and his men loaded them on bull boats and floated them down the Big Horn and Yellowstone rivers to the Missouri River. Near where

Traders sometimes camped with Indians to buy buffalo hides and furs.

Mountain men and Indians attended annual rendezvous, where they traded furs for items such as rifles, knives, tools, traps, blankets, shirts, sugar, flour, and coffee. The first rendezvous lasted one day, but others lasted as long as several weeks.

the Yellowstone and Missouri rivers meet, soldiers waited to escort Ashley's group and their furs to St. Louis by boat.

The first mountain man rendezvous was over, but there would be 15 more. This was the only time the furs were taken to St. Louis by water, however. All the other furs would be transported over land by way of the Great Fur Trade Road, later called the Oregon Trail.

During the fall of 1825, Bridger and other trappers hunted beaver. When they returned to Cache Valley, they stored the furs and prepared for winter. That winter was severely cold and snowy, so the men moved south near present-day Ogden, Utah, to a slightly milder climate. This area became winter quarters for the mountain men.

In the spring of 1826, Bridger trapped in Cache Valley and prepared for the next fur-trading rendezvous. When the supply caravan arrived, the mountain men greeted it with singing, dancing, and shouting. A Missouri newspaper wrote about Bridger and the other trappers:

> *[They] have been out four or five years, and are too happy in the freedom of those wild regions to think of returning to ... civilized life.*

*Mountain Man
Rendezvous Sites*

1825–*Henry's Fork
near McKinnon, Wyo.*
1826–*Willow Valley
(Cache Valley), Utah*
1827, 1828–*Bear Lake
near Laketown, Utah*
1829, 1832–*Pierre's
Hole near Driggs, Idaho*
1830, 1838–*Wind River
near Riverton, Wyo.*
1831–*Cache Valley
(but supply train did
not arrive)*
1833, 1835, 1836,
1837, 1839, 1840–
Near Daniel, Wyo.
1834–*Near Granger,
Wyo.*

During the 1826 rendezvous, Ashley sold his fur company to Jedediah Smith and his partners. Now Bridger worked for the new owners as a brigade leader.

At the end of the rendezvous, Bridger and fellow trapper Thomas Fitzpatrick led their brigade to what is now Yellowstone National Park. They were

Yellowstone National Park in Wyoming, Montana, and Idaho is famous for its hot springs and geysers. It is home to bison, elk, grizzly bears, and wolves.

captivated by waterfalls "leaping and thundering down the precipices," geysers that "spout up seventy feet [21 meters], with a terrible hissing noise, at regular intervals," and "great springs, so hot that meat is readily cooked in them." Bridger knew he would return to this wonderland, and he did many times.

After visiting the Yellowstone area, Bridger described his discoveries to others. Some of his stories about the land were so remarkable that people didn't believe him. So Bridger decided he might as well exaggerate the truth. One of his tales involved a petrified forest with petrified birds singing petrified songs. He did see petrified forests with fossilized tree trunks, leaves, twigs, needles, and cones in Yellowstone. But the petrified birds and songs were his own additions.

Bridger also told a story about an ice-cold spring that flowed down the mountain and moved so fast that its water became hot at the bottom. No one believed him, but years later, another explorer set up camp near Firehole River in Yellowstone's geyser and hot springs area. Taking off his boots and socks, he waded across. In the middle of the stream, he felt a warm sensation under his feet and discovered he was standing over a hot spring vent. He realized this may have been the river Bridger said was hot at the bottom.

During the summers of 1827 and 1828, Bridger attended the mountain man rendezvous at what came to be called Bear Lake on the Utah-Idaho border. For many years, Indians had enjoyed Bear Lake's sandy beaches and clear

Mountain men spun yarns around the camp-fire, and Jim Bridger was one of the best. As a guide or scout, Bridger was exact with his facts. But when he swapped yarns, he used his imagina-tion—and peppered his stories with facts. He told tales with a serious expression and laughed when listeners fell into his trap. Since Bridger did not read or write, he used the oral tradition of storytelling and relied on others to record his tales.

turquoise waters. Now white trappers also admired the picturesque landscape and enjoyed the mild, short summers in what is now Bear Lake Valley.

The following year, a supply train brought a new trapper near present-day Lander, Wyoming. Joseph Meek was 19 years old, inexperienced, and much

Joseph Meek learned about trapping from Bridger and other mountain men.

like Bridger when he first entered the mountains. The trappers and traders took Meek to the 1829 rendezvous at a place called Pierre's Hole near today's Idaho-Wyoming border. There they taught Meek about telling boastful tales, racing horses, and participating in shooting matches and high-spirited activities.

Soon it was time to head to fall trapping grounds, and the men organized their teams. Bridger took his brigade into Blackfeet Indian territory. Several years earlier, this tribe had been hostile to Henry-Ashley's men. Things hadn't changed. When Bridger entered Blackfeet land, one of the Indians shot at him and hit his horse. The animal reared and pitched, causing Bridger to drop his rifle. The Indian grabbed the gun, and Bridger rode away on his wounded horse.

About this time, some of the mountain men gave Bridger a nickname—Old Gabe. There were several stories about how he got the name. One account was that Jedediah Smith watched Bridger talk to his men and compared him to the angel Gabriel in the

Joseph L. Meek (1810–1875) was the son of a Virginia plantation owner. After his mother died and his father remarried, Meek left home. He worked with his brother in Missouri until he joined a fur trading company in 1829. Meek lived in the mountains for 12 years and often traveled with Bridger. When the fur trade died, he helped settle Oregon and became a territorial sheriff, farmer, family man, and storyteller.

Bible. Just as Gabriel brought a message from God, so Bridger ordered his men around with authority. Someone else suggested that Bridger's solemn expression must have been like Gabriel's when he foretold future events. People said Bridger looked as though the end of the world might come soon. Whatever the reason, the nickname Old Gabe stuck.

In 1830, at the age of 26, Bridger became a business owner. He and four others purchased Smith's fur business and named it the Rocky Mountain Fur Company. Other trappers, however, swarmed into the region and gave them stiff competition. Bridger's new business would last only four years.

When the wealthy American Fur Company moved into the area in 1832, it started gobbling up Rocky Mountain's profits. Knowing that Bridger knew the land well, trappers with the American Fur Company followed Bridger and his men to their fall trapping grounds. But Bridger purposely led them into hostile Blackfeet country. The Indians attacked the American Fur trappers and wounded or killed several of them.

In the meantime, so the story goes, Bridger set off on his own. When he came upon a group of Blackfeet Indians, the chief of the tribe held out his hand in friendship. But Old Gabe saw a movement among the other Indians and cocked his rifle. The chief heard the click, grabbed the gun, and knocked Bridger to

the ground. During the struggle, one of the Blackfeet shot an arrow into Bridger's back. Although the arrow was removed, the arrowhead wedged deep into his flesh and would remain there for three years. 🐾

For the most part, Bridger had good relations with the Indian tribes in the West.

5 OLD GABE STARTS A FAMILY

❧⤳❧

In 1835, it was time for the 11th mountain man rendezvous. A supply wagon train arrived at the site near present-day Daniel, Wyoming. Among the travelers was Dr. Marcus Whitman. Bridger told Whitman about his scuffle with the Blackfeet chief and showed him the arrowhead in his back. The doctor went to his wagon to get his surgical tools.

Without using any medicine to ease Bridger's pain, Whitman operated on Bridger. The 3-inch (7.6-centimeter) arrowhead had lodged into a large bone, and tissue had grown around it. The Rev. Samuel Parker, another train member, wrote, "The Doctor pursued the operation with great self-possession and perseverance; and his patient manifested equal firmness." Indians who watched

Bridger's first wife was Cora, daughter of Flathead Indian Chief Insala.

the operation were astonished when Whitman pulled out the arrowhead.

A week after the surgery, Bridger was ready to guide a group of missionaries to Little Jackson Hole near the Teton Mountains. It was against their religious beliefs to travel on Sunday. Instead, they held religious services and invited their guides and a group of Indians to attend. Joseph Meek wrote, "A scene more unusual could hardly have transpired than that of a company of trappers listening to the preaching of the word of God."

The Indian guests seemed interested in Parker's preaching. The trappers, however, "were as politely

Some of the many settlers who headed West were missionaries, who wanted to bring their religious beliefs to the Indian tribes.

attentive as it was in their reckless natures to be." In the middle of the sermon, a band of buffalo appeared. The congregation "broke up, without staying for a benediction" and left the minister "to discourse [talk] to vacant ground."

When Bridger's brigade had taken the missionaries where they wanted to go, the men trekked to the mountains to trap and explore. A friendship had formed between Bridger and Flathead Indian Chief Insala. Some of the tribe went with Bridger's group to hunt for their winter supply of buffalo. About this time, Bridger married Insala's daughter Cora.

According to Bridger, the Flatheads were good, ambitious people. Now, as Chief Insala's son-in-law, Bridger became a prominent member of their tribe. Cora made him a multicolored blanket to wear on special occasions. The Flatheads and the Crows then started calling him Blanket Chief. Bridger learned the customs and languages of several Indian tribes. He also became an expert communicator by using hand gestures. All the tribes could understand what he was saying with his hand movements.

> *The Flatheads lived in western Montana near the head of the Missouri River. A good-natured tribe, they were enemies of the more hostile Blackfeet. The Flatheads hunted buffalo for food and clothing, and they made living quarters called lodges from buffalo hides. In 1855, this tribe was placed on an Indian reservation in Montana.*

When the rendezvous of 1836 met near Daniel, Wyoming, Bridger showed off his new wife, Cora. He also proudly presented their infant daughter Mary Ann. She rode in a cradleboard on Cora's back.

To everyone's surprise that year, the supply train arrived with two white women. They were the wives of Presbyterian missionaries Dr. Marcus Whitman and Dr. Henry Spalding. Bridger again welcomed Whitman to the rendezvous. He remembered well the doctor who had removed the arrowhead from his back the year before.

In her diary, Spalding's wife, Eliza, wrote, "Arrived at the Rendezvous this evening. Were met by a large party of Nez Perces, men, women, and children. The women were not satisfied short of saluting Mrs. W. [Whitman] and myself with a kiss. All appear happy to see us." For 12 days the missionaries rested their animals and regained their own strength. Then they set out to continue their journey.

The next summer, more than 2,000 traders, trappers, and Indians met for the 1837 rendezvous near Daniel, Wyoming. This time, the supply caravan brought Sir William Drummond Stewart, a provost, or type of mayor, from Scotland. A young artist named Alfred Jacob Miller accompanied him to sketch scenes of the rendezvous and the West. One of Miller's first drawings showed a parade of Snake Indians welcoming the wagon train. The artist also

Jim Bridger (left) with Sir William Drummond Stewart

sketched Bridger in a knight's suit of armor riding his horse. Stewart knew Bridger from previous rendezvous and brought the armor as a gift for his trapper friend.

David Brown was another passenger on the wagon train. He noted that Bridger had a thorough understanding of the Indian character and described his skills:

> *[His] bravery was unquestionable, his horsemanship equally so, and as to his skill with the rifle ... he had been known to kill twenty buffaloes by the same number of consecutive shots.*

According to Brown, Bridger put his faith in Indian superstitions. "To complete the picture," he said, "he was perfectly ignorant of all knowledge contained in books, not even knowing the letters of the alphabet." But Bridger believed it took more than book learning to be a first-rate mountain man.

By 1839, Bridger was planning a trip to Missouri. After 17 years in the mountains, he was going home for the first time. He left Cora and 3-year-old Mary Ann with their Flathead kin and headed east. When he reached St. Louis, he was shocked at what he saw. Houses had sprung up, and hotels and boardinghouses were full. More than 150 steamships regularly delivered cargo to a city of 16,000 people. Bridger entered the city with his beard and his buckskin jacket. There were no beaver traps or mountain streams here. He got lost on the streets he once knew so well. When he told people about the amazing West, they thought he was lying.

While he was in St. Louis, Bridger met a Catholic priest named Father

Father Pierre Jean De Smet was a Catholic priest and missionary to the people of the U.S. frontier.

Pierre Jean De Smet. When a supply caravan left in 1840 to go West, De Smet, a group of missionaries, and Bridger went with it. They were on their way to the 1840 mountain man rendezvous. De Smet would eventually make many trips West and would become Jim Bridger's lifelong friend.

Bridger left the wagon train for a while to go get Cora and Mary Ann, who was now 4. Bridger brought his family back, and they headed to the rendezvous near Daniel, Wyoming. At the rendezvous, De Smet reported that the Shoshones were present in great numbers. "They gave a parade to greet the whites that were there," he wrote. "After riding a few times around the camp, ... they dismounted and all came to shake hands with the whites in sign of friendship."

Not as many trappers and traders were attending the rendezvous now. Most of the beavers had been trapped, and beaver hats were now out of style. Supply caravans were no longer as profitable as they once were, so the traders announced that this was the last rendezvous.

Father Pierre Jean De Smet (1801–1873) moved from Belgium to St. Louis to do missionary work. He made his first trip to the Rocky Mountains in 1840, where he attended the last mountain man rendezvous. De Smet traveled West several times to "Christianize" Native Americans, participate in peace conferences, and make geographical descriptions and maps. In Missouri, he later baptized some of Bridger's children and offered them an education.

Chapter

6 LIFE AT FORT BRIDGER

⚬⚬⚬

Without the summer rendezvous, there was no supply caravan in 1841. But a group of settlers did go West that year. An independent company left Westport, Missouri, with De Smet, some missionaries, a few pioneer families, and Thomas Fitzpatrick as their guide. One of their covered wagons broke down not far from Bridger's settlement in southwestern Wyoming. While they waited for repairs, Fitzpatrick and De Smet paid a visit to their friend Old Gabe.

Bridger was now 37 years old. His daughter Mary Ann was 5, and Bridger decided she should get an education. He wanted her to go to a school Dr. Whitman had established in the Oregon Territory. It wasn't long before the little girl was attending the Whitman Mission school near present-day Walla Walla, Washington. Whitman's wife wrote, "Mary Ann is of a mild disposition and easily governed and makes but little trouble."

That summer, Bridger and a partner began constructing a small fort on the Green River. Emigrants might need to replace food, worn-out blankets, and animals, and the fort could supply them with what they needed. Before the fort was finished, however, Bridger's partner was killed by Indians. The fort was never completed.

In December 1841, Cora gave birth to their second child, a son named Felix Francis. Bridger was now building a second fort in southwestern Wyoming. When his friend Fitzpatrick stopped by on his way back East, Old Gabe's mind turned toward Missouri.

Louis Vasquez helped Bridger build Fort Bridger.

He left his family and his unfinished fort and joined Fitzpatrick and a caravan full of furs.

Once again in St. Louis, Bridger now formed some sort of partnership with a man named Louis Vasquez. It wasn't long before they were in southwestern Wyoming building a fort where the Black's Fork River divided into several streams. Aspen trees provided shade, and grass grew abundantly there. The snowcapped Uinta Mountains offered a scenic backdrop. In 1843, the two men hastily constructed what they called Fort Bridger.

Bridger dictated a letter that described his new trading post:

> I have established a small store with a Black Smith Shop, and a supply of iron in the road of the Emigrants, on Black's Fork ... . They [the travelers] ... are generally well supplied with money, but by the time they get there, are in want of all kinds of supplies.

Two years later, a pioneer who was camping near Fort Bridger described it this way:

> It is a shabby concern. Here are about twenty-five lodges of Indians, or rather white trappers' lodges occupied by their Indian wives. They have a good supply of robes, dressed deer, elk and antelope skins, coats, pants, moccasins, and other Indian fixens, which they trade low for flour, pork, powder, lead, blankets, butcher-knives, spirits, hats, ready made clothes, coffee, sugar.

Louis Vasquez (1798–1868) was the youngest of 12 children born to prominent parents in St. Louis. He attended school in St. Louis and became part of the Missouri fur trade. Almost every year, he traveled back and forth between the mountains and St. Louis. He established Fort Vasquez and, as Bridger's partner, constructed and operated Fort Bridger. In St. Louis, Vasquez married a widow with two small children and then took his family West and expanded his business and his family. Vasquez later retired in Missouri.

During the first four years, Bridger and Vasquez did little to improve Fort Bridger. Travelers seldom found Old Gabe at home, since he was out trapping or exploring. His travels now included the southwestern, western, and northwestern parts of the country.

In about 1846 at Fort Bridger, Cora gave birth to a daughter—Mary Josephine. But soon afterward, Cora died. No one knows who took care of Felix and Mary Josephine. Mary Ann was still attending the Whitman Mission school in Oregon. She lived with Joseph Meek's daughter, Helen.

Fort Bridger, Wyoming, along the Oregon Trail, was a popular stopping place for pioneers headed West.

The following year, Vasquez got married in St. Louis and then moved with his new bride to Fort Bridger. As usual, Old Gabe was out on the trail. On one of his trips, he met a man by the name of Brigham Young. He was the leader of a religious group called Mormons and was planning to settle in the valley by the Great Salt Lake. Even though Bridger called this valley his paradise, he warned Young that cold weather might affect the crops. In spite of Bridger's concern, Young believed this was the right place to settle.

Travelers who stopped at Fort Bridger didn't always bring good news. In April 1848, Joseph Meek stopped at Fort Bridger on his way to Washington, D.C. He and his company had come from the Northwest with terrible news. During the fall of 1847, pioneers had arrived there, and some of them were sick with measles. Many Cayuse Indians in the area caught the disease and died. Someone at the Whitman Mission started spreading lies that Dr. Whitman was poisoning the tribe.

On November 29, in the mis-

Between 1840 and 1870, more than 70,000 Mormon pioneers crossed the plains to Utah. They were members of The Church of Jesus Christ of Latter-day Saints, founded by Joseph Smith in 1830 in New York. Church headquarters moved to Ohio, Missouri, and then Illinois. After Joseph Smith was killed and Brigham Young became the church's leader, the headquarters moved to Utah. By settling in Utah, Mormons hoped to be sheltered from religious persecution they had previously experienced.

sion's living room, Meek's daughter Helen and two other girls lay seriously ill with measles. Mary Ann Bridger was in the kitchen washing dishes from the noonday meal, when several Indians walked into the kitchen and asked for Dr. Whitman. When the doctor entered the room, the Indians shot him with a rifle.

Terrified, Mary Ann fled outside, ran around the house, and burst into the living room. Narcissa

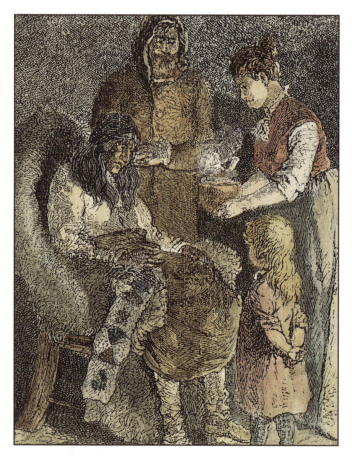

Narcissa Whitman tended to a sick Cayuse Indian at the Whitman Mission, located about 7 miles (11.2 km) west of present-day Walla Walla, Washington.

Whitman grabbed the child and questioned her about her husband. After the Indians left the house, Mrs. Whitman and three other women pulled Dr. Whitman into the living room and tried to stop his bleeding. As Narcissa walked over to the window, an Indian outside shot and wounded her. Seven adults and six girls sought safety in an upstairs room. When the attackers threatened to torch the mission house, the adults went to a nearby house. Narcissa and one of the men were shot and killed when they went outside. By the time the attack was over, the Cayuse Indians had killed 13 people, including Dr. Whitman, who died later that day.

The sick children were still in the mission house. Since no one came back for them, 13-year-old Catherine Sager stayed with them all night. "We sat on the bed hardly daring to breathe in our fright. I took all the children on one bed." The next morning, she and Elizabeth Sager carried their two ill sisters to another house. Mary Ann was at their side. When Catherine returned for 10-year-old Helen, she "was crying as though her heart would break, for she thought she had been left." Helen died on December 8.

Bridger later learned that Mary Ann had died in March. Now Bridger had lost his wife and his oldest daughter. Sometime during the next year, Bridger remarried. Her name was Chipta-Virginia, a woman from the Ute Indian tribe. A traveler visiting Fort Bridger in 1849 wrote that Bridger lived with his Indian wife in one of the log huts.

The traveler went on to describe the other buildings at the fort:

> *M. Vasquez' family occupied another, a third was a store, and the fourth contained a good forge and a rude carpenter's shop. ... Mr. Bridger ... was in the habit of leaving his partner as the home manager and spending a great deal of his time in roaming through the ... wilderness.*

A pioneer from another train also described the fort:

> *Opening upon a court were the rooms occupied by the Bridger family. ... In a corner of Mrs. Bridger's room was a churn filled with buttermilk, and dipping from it with a ladle, Mrs. Vasquez filled and refilled our cups, which we drank until completely satisfied.*

On July 4, 1849, Chipta-Virginia gave birth to a baby girl. They named her Virginia. Nine days later, Chipta-Virginia died, leaving her husband with three children to care for. As an adult, Virginia would one day write that her father took "responsibility on himself for the care of me when I was a little babe, he give me Buffalo and mare milk in a bottle."

As a young child, Virginia often sat on the wall at Fort Bridger waiting for her father to return from hunting. When she saw him coming, she jumped down and ran through the fort to meet him. One time in her excitement, she stepped in a blacksmith's fire and burned her foot. Bridger carried his daughter to the river and soaked her foot to peel off the moccasin.

An 1875 photograph of Jim Bridger's daughter Virginia Bridger Wachsman (1849–1933)

Another time, the Utes kidnapped young Virginia and hid her inside a tepee. Bridger searched for her in the Indian camp. When Virginia heard her father's voice outside the tepee, she crawled out and grabbed him around his knees. He lifted his daughter onto his horse and carried her home.

Bridger spent much of his time away from home. Others would care for his offspring. His business was in the mountains. ❧

7 Chapter

COMMUNICATING WITH THE TRIBES

❧

By now, Bridger had quite a good reputation as a scout and trailblazer. The West had been his home for nearly 30 years, and he knew it well. In 1850, Captain Howard Stansbury, an engineer for the U.S. Army, asked Bridger to guide his expedition. Old Gabe left his children at Fort Bridger and headed out on the trail.

Stansbury's task was to find a new route across Wyoming that would take them to the Great Salt Lake region. A better path would reduce travel time for the heavy wagons that brought pioneers to the Pacific Coast. Bridger suggested going across southern Wyoming. He sketched the course on paper and led Stansbury's party in that direction.

Their trip had plenty of adventure. Along the

Chief Washakie of the Shoshone Indian tribe was Bridger's father-in-law.

Indians and white men sometimes held councils to work out their differences.

trail, a band of Sioux Indian scouts approached Stansbury's men. Bridger shouldered his rifle and walked out to meet them. The Indians, who were not hostile, came to Stansbury's camp and held out their hands in friendship.

Although Bridger didn't know the Sioux language, he used gestures to communicate with the Indians. Stansbury reported:

> [Bridger] held the whole circle, for more than an hour, ... most deeply interested in a conversation and narrative, the whole of which was carried on without the utterance of a single word. The

simultaneous exclamations of surprise or interest, and the occasional bursts of hearty laughter, showed that the whole party perfectly understood.

Stansbury soon realized that Bridger's "language of signs is universally understood by all the tribes." Bridger's communication skills had made the Indians their friends. His excellent scouting skills were also proving to be very useful. He would lead Stansbury's group on a path that would one day be the route for the Overland Stage and the Transcontinental Railroad.

It wasn't long before Bridger got married again. About 1850, he married his third wife, young Mary Little Fawn. She was the daughter of Shoshone Chief Washakie, who was about the same age as Bridger. Now Felix, Mary Josephine, and Virginia had a mother to care for them again. Sometime around 1851, Bridger and Mary Little Fawn had a son named John.

Fort Bridger was an interesting place to raise a family, but Bridger wanted his children to have a formal education. They couldn't get that where they were. So in 1852, he

Chief Washakie (c. 1804–1900) was a great warrior and chief of the Shoshone tribe in Wyoming. A friend to pioneers, he believed people should work together peacefully. Washakie assisted the U.S. Army against hostile Indian tribes. His granting of a right-of-way through Shoshone land allowed the Transcontinental Railroad to be completed in 1869.

sent 10-year-old Felix and 6-year-old Mary Josephine to school in St. Charles, Missouri. Bridger's good friend Father De Smet wrote:

> *Captain Bridger, an old Rocky Mountain friend of mine, has sent his two children ... to be educated. ... He has left means with Colonel Robert Campbell for their education and clothing.*

Many important people stopped at Fort Bridger on their way West. In October 1852, Benjamin Ferris, the new Secretary of Utah Territory, and his wife stopped by on their way to Utah. Bridger invited them in and introduced them to his wife and children. Virginia was 3, and John was a toddler. Mrs. Ferris called them "keen, bright-eyed little things." She described 48-year-old Jim Bridger as "the oldest trapper in the Rocky Mountains; his language is very graphic and descriptive, and he is evidently a man of great shrewdness."

Old Gabe warned the couple about going to Utah so late in the season. He said "the season had arrived when a heavy snow might be looked for any day." After suggesting they spend the winter at Fort Bridger, Mrs. Ferris told how he "showed us where we could lodge, guarded against the cold with plenty of buffalo skins." Mary Little Fawn "exhibited some curious pieces of Indian embroidery, the work of her

own hands," and gave Mrs. Ferris raisins and berries. But Ferris wanted to keep traveling, and Bridger urged his guests to leave right away if they must go. He packed fresh potatoes and other vegetables for them to take, and the couple proceeded to Utah. It was an extremely cold winter that year, and the snowfall was heavy. 🕮

By the 1870s, Salt Lake City, Utah, would become an established city with homes, businesses, churches, and schools.

Chapter

8 THE CALL OF THE WEST

∽◦◦◦◦∾

By 1853, Bridger had made a major change in his life. He bought a farm in Jackson County, Missouri. Daughter Virginia wrote, "Father had 375 acres under cultivation, and several hundred more in timber." The family lived in a log house until Bridger could finish a two-story frame home on the property.

Bridger's farm was about 10 miles (16 km) south of Westport, now Kansas City, Missouri. Westport began as a place for travelers to purchase wagons and supplies for their journey westward. The town now had gristmills, sawmills, blacksmith shops, wagon-making shops, grocery and supply stores, and a large hotel. But Bridger still felt the call of the West. Not long after the move, he rented out his farmland, left his family behind, and returned to the mountains.

The Wind River Mountain Range is located in what is now called Bridger Wilderness, Wyoming.

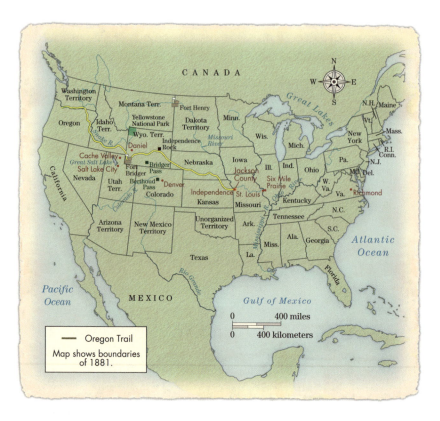

Bridger lived in Six Mile Prairie, Illinois, as a child and later bought a farm in Jackson County, Missouri. But for most of his life, he scouted the uncharted wilderness of the American frontier.

While he was gone, 49-year-old Jim Bridger became a father again. His daughter Mary Elizabeth was born in Missouri in 1853, at the same time Old Gabe was facing trouble in the West. The Fort Bridger area had become part of Utah Territory, and Mormon leaders heard that Bridger was distributing guns and ammunition to Indians to use against the Mormons. Whether this was true or not, territory authorities took away his trading license and authorized his arrest. Bridger returned to Missouri before he could be arrested. It was then that he saw Mary Elizabeth for the first time.

That October, Father De Smet wrote to Bridger about a visit he paid to Felix and Mary Josephine.

> *They appeared to be well pleased and are certainly well taken care of. Felix frequents our school and is making progress. His sister lives in the Academy and under the immediate care of the Ladies of that well-conducted establishment. ... Both have been somewhat sickly during the winter, but are now doing well.*

In 1854, Bridger sent two more of his children—5-year-old Virginia and her younger brother John—to St. Louis with Robert Campbell. After the children reached St. Louis, Virginia recalled, "I wanted to go back to my father. I cryed myself sick and my aunt done all she could to quite [quiet] me, but I soon got over my scare." Virginia lived with the Campbell family until she entered a Catholic school later in nearby St. Charles. That year, De Smet baptized Virginia and John. No one is sure what happened to John or Mary Josephine after their early years in Missouri.

For the next two years, Bridger worked off and on for Sir George Gore, a wealthy Irishman. Gore had organized an elaborate sportsman's

Robert Campbell (1804–1879) worked with Jim Bridger between 1825 and 1835. He led fur brigades and helped establish several trading posts, including Fort William—the first Fort Laramie—in present-day Wyoming. In St. Louis, he became a successful banker, merchant, and real estate speculator.

hunting expedition in the mountains, and Bridger served as his guide. Gore's daily routine appeared peculiar to the seasoned mountain man. Gore slept until midmorning, bathed, ate breakfast, and then went on his daily hunt. Around 10 P.M., he returned, ate dinner, and read a book. After hunting for two years, the Irishman collected the heads of 40 grizzly bears, 2,500 buffalo, and many deer, elk, and antelope.

Old Gabe now spent most of his time on the trail. He often traveled back to Missouri, returning to the West probably each spring when the weather was warmer. Neither Bridger nor his partner Vasquez resided at Fort Bridger anymore. In 1849, Vasquez had opened a business in Salt Lake City and then sold it in 1855 when he moved to Missouri. That same year, Bridger and Vasquez had sold Fort Bridger to the Mormons for $8,000. The new owners made the first payment of $4,000, took possession of the fort, and began making improvements. Three years later, Vasquez received the final payment.

In 1857, U.S. President James Buchanan appointed a replacement for Brigham Young, the governor of the Utah Territory. Bridger met the new governor and 2,500 Army troops at Fort Laramie to guide them to Utah. Young had not been told he was being replaced. When he learned about the troops on their way to Mormon territory, he became concerned. He thought they might harm his people for their religious beliefs.

To delay the approaching Army, Mormons living in the Fort Bridger vicinity burned down the fort's wooden buildings and then returned to Utah.

When Bridger and the military train reached Fort Bridger, they found it in ruins. It was November and too late to go to Utah. So they set up winter quarters a few miles south of the destroyed fort, at Camp Scott. Many of the soldiers' horses starved or froze to death that winter.

Brigham Young (1801–1877) was the second leader of The Church of Jesus Christ of Latter-day Saints, also known as Mormons.

When spring 1858 arrived, the troops moved on to Utah. Bridger led them through Salt Lake City, which was almost completely deserted. Only a select group of men remained to torch the city if the Army tried to occupy their homes. The Mormons had originally come to Utah Territory because they were forced to leave their homes and property in other states over conflicts with their non-Mormon neighbors. Now they refused to let anyone take what they had worked so hard to build in the West.

Bridger led the Army through the empty city and traveled 40 miles (64 km) southwest without incident.

Then the Mormon residents quietly returned home. His service completed, 53-year-old Bridger headed back to Missouri and to a 1-year-old son named William. He would be Old Gabe's last child.

In 1859, Captain William Raynolds of the U.S. Army Corps of Engineers hired Bridger to lead his team of scientists. They were going to the region Old Gabe had explored as a young man—the Big Horn Valley in present-day South Dakota. Raynolds wrote, "My American guide, Bridger, is now on familiar ground and appears to be entirely at home in this country." Raynolds later noted that "Bridger's skill with the rifle soon added two [buffalo] cows to our larder." Fresh meat had been scarce for these men.

As winter approached, Bridger set up camp for Raynolds' team in some abandoned huts near present-day Glenrock, Wyoming. With shelters for protection and supplies at nearby Fort Laramie, life was easier than it had been when Bridger first arrived in the mountains. Yet, as Raynolds said, "there were many weary hours in winter quarters, when we longed for the social enjoyments of home and civilized life." To pass the time, the men recounted "incidents of adventure in life on the plains which had come to our ears," including stories Bridger told them.

In the spring of 1860, the Raynolds party proceeded westward to explore what is now Yellowstone National Park. Captain Raynolds desperately wanted to visit this wonderland, and Bridger was eager to prove his facts about geysers, bubbling mudpots, and hot springs. He was tired of people calling his tales "Jim Bridger's lies."

On the last day of May, the men found themselves floundering in deep snow. Even Bridger "lost heart and declared it would be impossible to go farther." By June 5, "the mud became practically impassable." Raynolds "counted at one time twenty-five mules plunged deep in the mud." The captain fought tight deadlines and hunger and discouragement from his men. Bridger and Raynolds abandoned their plan to go to Yellowstone.

For more than a year, Old Gabe guided Raynolds' team. When Bridger returned to Missouri in the fall of 1860,

In the early 1870s, several parties explored the Yellowstone region and learned that Jim Bridger told the truth about the area. Yellowstone National Park became the world's first national park in 1872. Its name came from the Yellowstone River. A Native American tribe called it Mi tsi a da zi, or "rock yellow river," because some of its banks contained high yellow rock cliffs. John Colter, a member of Lewis and Clark's expedition, was the first white man to visit the area.

Mary Little Fawn was not there to greet him. His wife had died the year before. According to public records, Bridger's children—Felix, Virginia, Mary Elizabeth, and William—were living with a woman named Ruth Scaggs and her two children in New Santa Fe, south of Westport. But even losing a wife couldn't stop Bridger from returning to his mountains.

9 TROUBLESOME YEARS

Chapter

᭒᭞᭒

Before heading West again, Bridger attended to his family's needs. He stored food, clothing, and other necessities. George London, his wife in Westport, and others took over the upbringing of Bridger's children as they grew and continued their education. Virginia remembered leaving St. Louis and enrolling in a Kansas City academy. She remembered, "I would ride my pony that Pa got for me down every morning to school and back."

On April 12, 1861, the Civil War began, and Missouri became a dangerous place. Virginia said, "Our big farmhouse was destroyed in the war, but later my father built a smaller one near the site." During the war, transportation companies, the U.S. Army, and emigrants crossing the Plains needed

In May 1861, just one month after the outbreak of the Civil War, Union Army volunteers were attacked in St. Louis, Missouri.

Bridger's skills. The Pony Express and the telegraph were helping people communicate across the country. Companies were demanding faster, safer ways to take goods West.

In 1861, Bridger guided Army Captain E.L. Berthoud's surveying crew to locate a better route between Denver and Salt Lake City. Bridger suggested going through what is now called Bridger's Pass in southern Wyoming. Instead, the surveyors chose what would be called Berthoud Pass in Colorado. Since this pass was at a higher elevation, Old Gabe

A Pony Express rider offered a friendly wave to workers raising telegraph poles in the West in 1860.

knew snow would close it in the winter. The surveyors had only seen Berthoud Pass in the summer, so they didn't know how treacherous it could be.

During the fall, Old Gabe returned to Missouri. In 1862, he escorted two federal judges and their families in a military wagon train to the Utah Territory. Near the Sweetwater River in present-day Wyoming, Indians attacked another group 5 miles (8 km) behind Bridger's, killed two men, and stole their horses. Bridger and others from the government train rushed to the scene and found a gruesome sight. They recovered the bodies and searched for the slayers without success. In spite of the tragedy, Bridger led the military train on to the Utah Territory.

Both Bridger's Pass and Berthoud Pass are located on the Continental Divide. Bridger's Pass is southwest of Rawlins, Wyoming, and Berthoud is west of Denver, Colorado. Bridger's Pass is 7,532 feet (2,297 m) above sea level, and Berthoud Pass is 11,314 feet (3,451 m) above. Today, Interstate 80 runs near Bridger's Pass, and U.S. Highway 40 crosses Berthoud Pass.

That year, Bridger also served as a guide for Colonel William Collins and his troops. Collins had been ordered to guard 500 miles (800 km) of trail in Wyoming. Indian warriors were raiding mail and telegraph stations and frightening emigrants. To preserve their lands and way of life, the Indians were reacting to broken treaties and life-threatening changes.

Eighteen-year-old Caspar Collins accompanied his father on this assignment. Intrigued by Bridger's mountain man habits, Caspar wrote:

The names of many mountain men were carved into Independence Rock in Wyoming along the Oregon Trail.

> *It was amusing to see old Major Bridger cooking his supper. He would take a whole jack rabbit and a trout about eighteen inches long and put them on two sticks and set them up before the fire and eat them both without a particle of salt and drink about a quart of strong coffee. He says when he was young he has often eaten the whole side ribs of a buffalo.*

Young Collins also observed Bridger's knowledge of the land and climate. Near Independence Rock, Collins said, "This is the worst country for winds I ever saw. ... Major Bridger, went off this morning up in the mountains to get out of the wind. He says he is going to get in some cañon [canyon] and make a large fire."

After Bridger completed his work with Collins, he spent the winter at Fort Laramie. In the spring of 1864, he led a wagon train to Montana to find gold. In northern Wyoming, the travelers came upon a band of Shoshone Indians. Old Gabe and a few other men approached the chief and his braves as they rode toward them. The Shoshones recognized their old friend and began shouting, "Bridger! Bridger!" The chief was Washakie, the father of Bridger's wife Mary Little Fawn. Train members prepared a feast and presented gifts to the Indians before continuing on to Montana.

While Old Gabe served as a guide and scout in the West, his children were growing up and moving forward with their lives. Felix joined the Union Army

Independence Rock in central Wyoming was a favorite stopping place for travelers. They climbed around it and carved their names on its rounded granite surface. Even though the Sweetwater River flowed nearby, some emigrants wondered if anything could grow in this barren land. According to a tall tale attributed to Bridger, he threw a stone across the Sweetwater when he first arrived, and it grew to be Independence Rock.

to fight in the Civil War, and Virginia married Albert Wachsman, a Union Army captain, on February 25, 1864. Wachsman had sent a letter to Bridger at Fort Laramie, asking for permission to marry his 14-year-old daughter. Virginia said, "Father thought I would be well taken care of, and he consented."

That October, a Civil War battle was fought at Westport, Missouri, just several miles north of

Confederate and Union soldiers clashed at the Civil War battle at Westport, Missouri.

Bridger's farm. Confederate General Sterling Price tried to take control of Missouri for the South at that battle. There were many wounded and killed— 1,500 on each side—in the Union victory. Virginia remembered when the soldiers came. The doctor in the community told the women, "Now ladies, I will have to press you into service as nurses." Virginia replied, "I am right here, ready, my husband might be out on that battlefield, and my brother, too." The hotel became a hospital, and Virginia served as a nurse for both Union and Confederate soldiers for about two weeks.

When Bridger finally returned to Missouri, he met his new son-in-law. He spent the winter with two of his children—Mary Elizabeth, who was now 11, and William, who was 8. After being gone for more than two years, Bridger noticed how they had changed. He needed to get to know them once again.

Albert Wachsman was married to Bridger's daughter Virginia.

In April 1865, the Civil War ended. But the war between the whites and the Indians persisted in the

West. The U.S. Army appointed General Grenville M. Dodge to stop the Indians who were raiding the westward trails. After a Cheyenne Indian village was brutally attacked in November, Indians sought revenge. Dodge asked General Patrick E. Conner from Denver to command a military unit, and he asked Old Gabe to act as scout and guide.

Grenville M. Dodge (1831–1916) was a Union Army officer on the frontier during the Civil War.

At 61 years old, Bridger took the job but didn't talk much with Conner's men. One of the soldiers remembered Bridger:

> [Bridger] would cook his frugal [small] meal, and as soon as darkness approached, wrap himself in his blankets for the night. But with the first peep of day he was astir, and after a hasty cup of coffee, and some jerked meat, he would saddle up, and after calling on General Conner, quietly ride away.

Bridger and General Dodge, however, became good friends. Besides preserving peace on the trail,

Dodge was designing a westward route for the Union Pacific Railroad. After studying the land, Dodge asked Bridger to show him the shortest and straightest route. As he had done for Stansbury's expedition 15 years earlier, Bridger now sketched out a course across southern Wyoming. In his written report for the railroad, Dodge said he was following Bridger's recommendations.

During the winter of 1865–1866, Bridger was again in Missouri. In February, he purchased a two-story building in Westport and opened a business to outfit wagons crossing the Plains. Then he headed West again to assist Dodge with his construction of the railroad. While Bridger was away, his son-in-law managed the store on the first floor of Bridger's building and a dance hall upstairs.

In his old age, Bridger's joints were stiffening with rheumatism, and his vision was no longer sharp. He would go to the mountains for the last time in 1868. Even though he eventually resigned himself to life in Missouri, Old Gabe's heart would always remain in the American West. ❧

10 THE END OF THE TRAIL

⤷⦿⤶

Jim Bridger finally settled down on his farm in Missouri. In 1871, he sold his store in Westport, and his son Felix came home to stay after serving in the military for eight years. Mary Elizabeth and William were teenagers now, and Virginia and her husband, Albert, had purchased a farm next to Bridger's.

With plenty of time on his hands, Old Gabe chatted with neighboring farmers who hauled their grain to Stubbins Watts' mill. The Watts and Bridger farms bordered each other, and the families were good friends. Lizzie, one of the Watts children, recalled a time when the old scout came to their house and angrily cussed at his horse. Lizzie said she had never heard such a fancy job of language. Later, Lizzie's little brother Edgar decided to talk to his pony that

Jim Bridger lived his final years in Missouri, but his heart was always in the American West.

way. But his mother disagreed and responded with a hearty spanking.

Sometimes neighbor children came to visit Bridger. One child later recalled:

> *He was always very hospitable and liked to have the children of the neighborhood come to visit him. ... He was proud of his apple orchard and used to send basketfuls of apples to his neighbors.*

Occasionally, friends attended dances at the Bridger home, where William played the violin and Virginia and Mary Elizabeth joined in the dancing.

As Bridger aged and his eyesight dimmed, he often sat on his porch with his chin on his cane, facing toward the West. By 1873, when his eyesight was almost gone, he could identify people only by their voices. He said, "I wish I was back there among the mountains again—you can see so much farther in that country."

Virginia remembered that her father "would get very nervous, and wanted to be on the go. I had to watch after him and lead him around to please him." She bought her father a gentle horse, which he named Ruff. As Bridger rode his horse around the farm, his devoted dog Sultan trotted beside them. Virginia recalled:

Father could not see very well, but the old faithful horse would guide him along, but at times father would draw the lines wrong, and the horse would go wrong, and then they would get lost in the woods. ... Sultan ... would let us know that father was lost. The dog would bark and whine until I would go out and look for him.

Bridger Mountains, named for Jim Bridger, are located on the Bozeman Trail in Montana.

Sometimes Bridger used his cane to walk to his wheat field, with Sultan by his side. To determine how high the wheat had grown, he would get down on his knees and feel the wheat with his hands.

In 1875, Virginia gave birth to a daughter, Louise, and Bridger became a grandfather. Though he was unable to see his granddaughter, he could hold her in his arms and hear her sounds. The new mother now looked after her newborn and her elderly father. Felix, Mary Elizabeth, and William also cared for their father. A year later, Felix Bridger died. The family buried him in the Watts Burying Ground near the Bridger farm.

Five years later, on July 17, 1881, Jim Bridger died at the age of 77. His children buried him in the Watts Burying Ground near his son Felix. Six years later, William also died and was laid to rest between his father and brother. Of Bridger's seven children, only Virginia and Mary Elizabeth married and had children.

Two decades after Bridger's death, General Dodge discovered that Bridger's grave had been neglected and almost forgotten. Dodge couldn't forget his friend. Old Gabe had been his guide in the West and laid out the route for the railroad through the Rocky Mountains. Dodge received permission to move Bridger's body to Mount Washington Cemetery in Independence, Missouri.

In a ceremony on December 11, 1904, Bridger's great-granddaughter, Mary Louise Lightle, unveiled a 7-foot (2-m) tombstone at his grave. Although by that time Dodge was ill and couldn't attend, his words were read at the event:

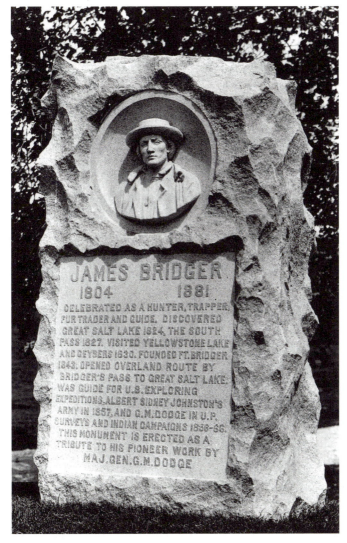

A large headstone memorializes Jim Bridger at his final resting place at Mount Washington Cemetery in Independence, Missouri.

93

I found Bridger a very companionable man. In person, he was over six feet tall, spare, straight as an arrow, agile, rawboned and of powerful frame, eyes gray, hair brown and abundant even in old age, expression mild and manners agreeable. He was hospitable and generous, and was always trusted and respected.

Dodge said Bridger was one of the most expert hunters and trappers in the mountains. With his keen ability to observe, he could describe with great accuracy places he had visited only once. Dodge also noted that the whole West was mapped out in his mind, and he could smell his way when he couldn't see it.

Jim Bridger's name will forever be connected to the old West. He will long be remembered for the mountains, lakes, and forests he explored. As an expert guide and scout, he brought people and businesses to new territories. He blazed trails for the military and found the best routes for wagons and railroads. His fort still bears his

Jim Bridger's name can be found at such locations as Fort Bridger, Bridger Mountains, Bridger Peak, Bridger Creek, Bridger Lake, Bridger Pass, Bridger Butte, Bridger National Forest, Utah's Cache Valley Bridgerland, and Bridger, Montana. Fort Bridger State Historic Site is 30 miles (48 km) east of Evanston, Wyoming, near Interstate 80. Each year on Labor Day weekend, Fort Bridger sponsors a mountain man rendezvous, which thousands of people attend.

WYOMING

OLD FORT BRIDGER
PIONEER TRADING POST

The fort was established about 1842 by Jim Bridger, discoverer of Great Salt Lake; notable pioneer, trapper, fur trader, scout and guide. Bridger was born at Richmond, Virginia, March 17, 1804 and died at Westport, Missouri, July 17, 1881. His unerring judgement regarding problems of trappers, traders, soldiers, emigrants and gold-seekers, bordered on the miraculous, and his advice was universally in demand in the early history of this state.

Bridger has been prominently recognized as America's greatest frontiersman and the west's most gifted scout.

name, but his true legacy is in the mountains, where this mountain man always returned and where he was most happy. ℘

In 1928, Fort Bridger was sold to the Wyoming Historic Landmark Commission to preserve the site as a historic monument.

BRIDGER'S LIFE

1804

Born in Richmond,
Virginia, March 17

1822

Signs up with
the Henry-Ashley
expedition

1825

Sees the
Great Salt Lake;
attends the first
mountain man
rendezvous

1820

1805

General
anesthesia
is first used
in surgery

1820

Susan B. Anthony,
American
suffragist, is born

1826

The first photo-
graph is taken by
Joseph Niépce, a
French physicist

WORLD EVENTS

1834 or 1835
Marries Cora, a
Flathead Indian

1843
Builds Fort
Bridger with
Louis Vasquez

1830
Buys the Rocky
Mountain Fur
Company with
his partners

1835

1828
Russian novelist
Leo Tolstoy is
born

1836
Texans defeat
Mexican troops
at San Jacinto
after a deadly
battle at the
Alamo, giving
Texas its
independence

1844
Samuel Morse
perfects the
telegraph

BRIDGER'S LIFE

1846
Wife Cora dies

1847
Meets the
first Mormon
wagon train on
its way to Utah

1848
Daughter Mary
Ann dies; marries
Chipta-Virginia

1846
German astronomer
Johann Gottfried
Galle discovers
Neptune

1848
*The Communist
Manifesto* by
German writer
Karl Marx is
widely distributed

WORLD EVENTS

1850

Marries Mary Little Fawn; guides the Stansbury expedition to the Great Salt Lake region

1849

Daughter Virginia is born; wife Chipta-Virginia dies

1853

Owns a farm in Missouri

1850

1850

Jeans are invented by Levi Strauss, a German who moved to California during the gold rush

1854

Japan opens its trade to the West after Commodore Matthew Perry arrives with gunships in Tokyo Bay

BRIDGER'S LIFE

1855

Sells Fort
Bridger

1857–1858

Guides Army
troops to Utah

1859

Wife Mary Little
Fawn dies

1860

1856

The Treaty of Paris
ends the Crimean War,
which was fought
between Russia and
the armies of Britain,
France, Sardinia, and
the Ottoman Empire

1858

English scientist
Charles Darwin
presents his the-
ory of evolution
to a gathering of
scientists

1859

*A Tale Of
Two Cities* by
Charles Dickens
is published

WORLD EVENTS

1868

Makes last trip West and retires in Missouri

1881

Dies at age 77 and is buried near his farm; body is moved to Independence, Missouri, 23 years later

1868

U.S. engineer Christopher L. Sholes invents the first practical typewriter

1876

Alexander Graham Bell makes the first successful telephone transmission

1881

Booker T. Washington founds Tuskegee Institute

DATE OF BIRTH: March 17, 1804

BIRTHPLACE: Richmond, Virginia

FATHER: James Bridger (?–1817)

MOTHER: Chloe Bridger (?–1816)

FIRST SPOUSE: Cora (Flathead tribe)
(?–1846)

DATE OF MARRIAGE: 1834 or 1835

CHILDREN: Mary Ann
(1835/1836–1848)
Felix Francis
(1841–1876)
Mary Josephine (1846–?)

SECOND SPOUSE: Chipta-Virginia
(Ute tribe)
(?–1849)

DATE OF MARRIAGE: About 1848

CHILDREN: Virginia (1849–1933)

THIRD SPOUSE: Mary Little Fawn
(Shoshone tribe)
(?–1859)

DATE OF MARRIAGE: About 1850

CHILDREN: John (1850 or 1851–?)
Mary Elizabeth
(1853–1922)
William (1857–1887)

DATE OF DEATH: July 17, 1881

PLACE OF BURIAL: Independence, Missouri

FURTHER READING

Janin, Hunt. *Fort Bridger, Wyoming: Trading Post for Indians, Mountain Men, and Westward Migrants.* Jefferson, N.C.: McFarland & Company, 2001.

Steber, Rick. *Mountain Men.* Prineville, Ore.: Bonanza Pub., 1990.

Sundling, Charles W. *Mountain Men of the Frontier.* Edina, Minn.: Abdo Publishing Co., 2000.

LOOK FOR MORE SIGNATURE LIVES BOOKS ABOUT THIS ERA:

James Beckwourth: *Mountaineer, Scout, and Pioneer*
ISBN 0-7565-1000-7

Crazy Horse: *Sioux Warrior*
ISBN 0-7565-0999-8

Geronimo: *Apache Warrior*
ISBN 0-7565-1002-3

Sam Houston: *Texas Hero*
ISBN 0-7565-1004-X

Jesse James: *Legendary Rebel and Outlaw*
ISBN 0-7565-1871-7

Bridget "Biddy" Mason: *From Slave to Businesswoman*
ISBN 0-7565-1001-5

Zebulon Pike: *Explorer and Soldier*
ISBN 0-7565-0998-X

Sarah Winnemucca: *Scout, Activist, and Teacher*
ISBN 0-7565-1003-1

ON THE WEB

For more information on *Jim Bridger*, use FactHound to track down Web sites related to this book.

1. Go to *www.facthound.com*
2. Type in this book ID: 0756518709
3. Click on the *Fetch It* button.

FactHound will find the best Web sites for you.

HISTORIC SITES

Fort Bridger State Historic Site
Box 35
Fort Bridger, WY 82933
307/782-3842
Original site of Fort Bridger, located 30 miles (48 km) east of Evanston, Wyoming; includes a museum and activities

Museum of the Mountain Man
Sublette County Historical Society Inc.
Box 909
700 E. Hennick
Pinedale, WY 82941
877/686-6266
Information about the fur trade and rendezvous in Wyoming

benediction
a blessing commonly spoken at the end of a religious meeting

brigade
a group of people organized for a special purpose

bull boat
a small boat that trappers built to navigate small rivers and streams

cache
a hidden place where something is stored

Confederate
Southern states and their military forces that fought against the Northern states during the Civil War

cradleboard
a wooden frame supporting a cloth enclosure for a baby, traditionally worn by Native American women

entrepreneurs
people who set up a business to make money

keelboats
covered river boats propelled by rowing, poling, or towing and often used for carrying freight

mountain men
trappers or fur traders who lived in and explored the American West searching for fur-bearing animals

rendezvous
a French word meaning a prearranged meeting; a meeting of the mountain men during the 1800s

Union
Northern states and their military forces that fought against the Southern states during the Civil War

Source Notes

Chapter 1

Page 10, line 18: J. Cecil Alter. *James Bridger: Trapper, Frontiersman, Scout and Guide: A Historical Narrative*. Columbus, Ohio: Long's College Book Co., 1951, p. 396.

Page 11, lines 1, 17: Ibid., p. 397.

Chapter 3

Page 23, line 5: Donald McKay Frost. *Notes on General Ashley: The Overland Trail and South Pass*. Barre, Mass.: Barre Gazette, 1960, p. 65.

Page 24, line 6: Ibid.

Page 28, line 19: Charles L. Camp., ed. *James Clyman: Frontiersman*. Portland, Ore.: Champoeg Press, 1960, p. 15.

Page 30, sidebar: Kenneth L. Holmes, and David Duniway. *Covered Wagon Women: Diaries & Letters from the Western Trails, 1840–1890* (Vol. 4), Spokane, Wash.: Arthur H. Clarke Company, 1991, p. 60.

Page 32, lines 11, 21: *Notes on General Ashley: The Overland Trail and South Pass*, p. 59.

Chapter 4

Page 39, line 16: *Notes on General Ashley: The Overland Trail and South Pass*, p. 138.

Page 40, line 1: J. Cecil Alter. *Jim Bridger*. Norman: University of Oklahoma Press, 1962, p. 77.

Chapter 5

Page 47, line 13: Samuel Parker. *Journal of an Exploring Tour Beyond the Rocky Mountains*. Ithaca, N.Y.: Mack, Andrus, & Woodruff, 1842. Reprinted Moscow, Idaho: University of Idaho Press, 1990, p. 80.

Page 48, line 8: Fred R. Gowans. *Rocky Mountain Rendezvous: A History of the Fur Trade Rendezvous, 1825–1840*. Provo, Utah: Brigham Young University Press, 1975, p. 158.

Page 48, line 13: Ibid.

Page 49, line 3: Ibid.

Page 50, line 12: Narcissa Whitman, and Eliza Spalding. *Where Wagons Could Go*. Lincoln: University of Nebraska Press, 1997, p. 194.

Page 51, line 9: David L. Brown. *Three Years in the Rocky Mountains*. Fairfield, Wash.: Ye Galleon Press, 1982, p. 16.

Page 52, line 2: Ibid.

Page 53, line 18: *Rocky Mountain Rendezvous: A History of the Fur Trade Rendezvous, 1825–1840*, p. 254.

Chapter 6

Page 56, line 2: Clifford M. Drury. *Marcus and Narcissa Whitman and the Opening of Old Oregon* (Vol. 1). Glendale, Calif.: The Arthur H. Clark Co., 1973, p. 406.

Page 57, line 8: *Jim Bridger*, p. 209.

Page 57, line 20: Joel Palmer. *Journal of Travels over the Rocky Mountains*. Ann Arbor, Mich.: University Microfilms, 1966, p. 35.

Page 61, line 17: Clifford M. Drury. *Marcus and Narcissa Whitman and the Opening of Old Oregon* (Vol. 2). Glendale, Calif.: The Arthur H. Clark Co., 1973, p. 239.

Page 61, line 22: Fred Lockley. *Conversations with Pioneer Women*. Eugene, Ore.: Rainy Day Press, 1981, p. 57.

Page 62, line 6: Ibid., pp. 205–206.

Page 62, line 14: Ibid., p. 208.

Page 62, line 25: Virginia Bridger Hahn. "The Life of Jim Bridger." Manuscript 204, Wyoming State Archives, Cheyenne, Wyoming, p. 3.

Chapter 7

Page 66, line 9: Howard Stansbury. *Exploration and Survey of the Valley of the Great Salt Lake of Utah*. Philadelphia: Lippincott, Grambo & Co., 1852, p. 254.

Page 67, line 5: Ibid.

Page 68, line 4: Hiram Martin Chittenden and Alfred Talbot Richardson. *Life, Letters and Travels of Father De Smet* (Vol. 4). New York: Arno Press, 1969, p. 1483.

Page 68, lines 15, 21: Mrs. B.G. Ferris. *The Mormons at Home*. New York: AMS Press, 1971, p. 84.

Chapter 8

Page 71, line 3: *Jim Bridger*, p. 240.

Page 73, line 3: *Life, Letters and Travels of Father De Smet* (Vol. 4), pp. 1484–1485.

Page 73, line 14: "The Life of Jim Bridger," p. 4.

Page 76, line 10: J. Cecil Alter. *James Bridger: Trapper, Frontiersman, Scout and Guide: A Historical Narrative*. Columbus, Ohio: Long's College Book Co., 1951, pp. 334, 342.

Page 76, line 20: Ibid., p. 355.

Page 77, line 8: Ibid., pp. 361, 363.

Chapter 9

Page 79, line 7: "Mountain Man's Daughter Returns to the Mountains—Reminisces." *Wind River Mountaineer*, January 1985, p. 14.

Page 79, line 12: "Bridger Daughter Dies." *Kansas City Star*, March 8, 1933. 8 September 2005. www.kclibrary.org/localhistory/media.cfm?mediaID=34533, p. 5.

Page 82, line 5: Agnes Wright Spring. *Caspar Collins: The Life and Exploits of an Indian Fighter of the Sixties*. New York: AMS Press, Inc., 1967, pp. 125–126.

Page 83, line 4: Ibid., pp. 116–117.

Page 84, line 5: "Mountain Man's Daughter returns to the Mountains—Reminisces," p. 15.

Page 85, line 6: Ibid., p. 14.

Page 86, line 19: *Jim Bridger*, p. 314.

Chapter 10

Page 90, line 5: *James Bridger: Trapper, Frontiersman, Scout and Guide: A Historical Narrative*, p. 480.

Page 90, line 17: *Jim Bridger*, p. 339.

Page 90, line 20: Grenville Mellen Dodge. *Biographical Sketch of James Bridger: Mountaineer, Trapper and Guide*. New York: Unz & Co., 1905, p. 23.

Page 91, line 1: Ibid.

Page 94, line 1: Ibid., p. 24.

Alter, J. Cecil. *James Bridger: Trapper, Frontiersman, Scout and Guide: A Historical Narrative*. Columbus, Ohio: Long's College Book Co., 1951.

Alter, J. Cecil. *Jim Bridger*. Norman: University of Oklahoma Press, 1962.

"Bridger Daughter Dies." *Kansas City Star*, March 8, 1933, p. 5. 8 September 2005. www.kclibrary.org/localhistory/media.cfm?mediaID=34533

Brown, David L. *Three Years in the Rocky Mountains*. Fairfield, Wash.: Ye Galleon Press, 1982.

Camp, Charles L., ed. *James Clyman: Frontiersman*. Portland, Ore.: Champoeg Press, 1960.

Chittenden, Hiram Martin, and Alfred Talbot Richardson. *Life, Letters and Travels of Father De Smet*, Vol. 4. New York: Arno Press, 1969.

Dodge, Grenville Mellen. *Biographical Sketch of James Bridger: Mountaineer, Trapper and Guide*. New York: Unz & Co., 1905.

Drury, Clifford M. *Marcus and Narcissa Whitman and the Opening of Old Oregon*. 2 vol. Glendale, Calif.: The Arthur H. Clark Co., 1973.

Ferris, Mrs. B. G. *The Mormons at Home*. New York: AMS Press, 1971.

Frost, Donald McKay. *Notes on General Ashley: The Overland Trail and South Pass*. Barre, Mass.: Barre Gazette, 1960.

Gowans, Fred R. *Rocky Mountain Rendezvous: A History of the Fur Trade Rendezvous, 1825-1840*. Provo, Utah: Brigham Young University Press, 1975.

Gowans, Fred R. Personal interviews. 19 January 2006 and 4 February 2006.

Hahn, Virginia Bridger. "The Life of Jim Bridger." Manuscript 204, Wyoming State Archives, Cheyenne, Wyoming.

Holmes, Kenneth L., and David Duniway. *Covered Wagon Women: Diaries & Letters from the Western Trails, 1840-1890* (12 vols.), Glendale, Calif./Spokane, Wash.: Arthur H. Clarke Company, 1983–1993.

Lockley, Fred. *Conversations with Pioneer Women*. Eugene, Ore.: Rainy Day Press, 1981.

"Mountain Man's Daughter Returns to the Mountains—Reminisces." Wind River Mountaineer, January 1985, pp. 12–16.

Palmer, Joel. *Journal of Travels over the Rocky Mountains*. Ann Arbor, Mich.: University Microfilms, 1966.

Parker, Samuel. *Journal of an Exploring Tour Beyond the Rocky Mountains*. Ithaca, N.Y.: Mack, Andrus, & Woodruff, 1842. Reprinted Moscow, Idaho: University of Idaho Press, 1990.

Spring, Agnes Wright. *Caspar Collins: The Life and Exploits of an Indian Fighter of the Sixties*. New York: AMS Press, Inc., 1967.

Stansbury, Howard. *Exploration and Survey of the Valley of the Great Salt Lake of Utah*. Philadelphia: Lippincott, Grambo & Co., 1852.

Whitman, Narcissa, and Eliza Spalding. *Where Wagons Could Go*. Lincoln: University of Nebraska Press, 1997.

American Fur Company, 44
American Revolution, 15
Arikara Indian tribe, 27, 29
Ashley, William Henry, 23–24, 26, 27, 28, 34, 37, 38, 39
Ashley's Hundred. *See* Henry-Ashley party.

Bear Lake, 32, 41–42
Bear River, 32, 34
beaver pelts, 19, 24, 30, 31–32, 38, 53
Beckwourth, Jim, 24
Berthoud, E.L., 80
Berthoud Pass, 80–81
Big Horn River, 30, 37
Big Horn Valley, 76
Blackfeet Indian tribe, 26, 43, 44–45, 47, 49
Brackett, William, 10–12
Bridger Butte, 94
Bridger, Chipta-Virginia (wife), 61–62
Bridger, Chloe (mother), 15, 16, 18
Bridger, Cora (wife), 49, 50, 53, 56
Bridger Creek, 94
Bridger, Felix Francis (son), 56, 58, 67, 68, 73, 77, 83–84, 89, 92
Bridger, James (father), 15, 16, 17, 18
Bridger, James "Jim"
  on Bear River expedition, 34
  birth of, 15
  as blacksmith's apprentice, 19, 21, 32
  as brigade leader, 39–40
  childhood of, 17
  as co-owner of Rocky Mountain Fur Company, 44
  communications skills of, 49, 66–67, 89
  death of, 92
  dog of, 90–91, 92
  education of, 13, 21, 52
  as explorer, 34, 58
  farm of, 71, 85, 89
  Fort Bridger and, 56–58, 59, 62–63, 67, 68, 72, 74, 75
  as fur trapper, 26, 31–32, 38, 39, 58
  as grandfather, 92
  at Great Salt Lake, 34
  Green River fort and, 56
  as guide, 9, 12–13, 31, 48, 65, 67, 74, 75, 76–77, 81, 83, 86
  health of, 45, 47, 87, 90
  in Henry-Ashley party, 24, 25, 26–27, 28, 30, 34
  horse of, 90–91
  Indian attacks and, 10–12, 43, 44–45, 47, 56, 63
  literacy of, 13, 21
  marriages of, 49, 61–62, 67
  as member of Flathead Indian tribe, 49
  Mississippi River and, 17–18
  nicknames of, 43–44, 49
  as orphan, 18–19
  as outfitter, 87
  at rendezvous, 32, 35, 37, 39, 41, 43, 47, 50, 53
  as scout, 31, 67, 86, 87
  siblings of, 16, 18
  sketches of, 51
  as storyteller, 41, 76, 83
  at winter quarters, 33, 39, 75, 76
  at Yellowstone, 39–41, 76–77
Bridger, John (son), 67, 68, 73
Bridger Lake, 94
Bridger, Mary Ann (daughter), 50, 53, 55–56, 58, 60, 61
Bridger, Mary Elizabeth (daughter), 72, 77, 85, 89, 90, 92
Bridger, Mary Josephine (daughter), 58, 67, 68, 73
Bridger, Mary Little Fawn (wife), 67, 68–69, 77
Bridger, Montana, 94
Bridger Mountains, 94
Bridger National Forest, 94
Bridger Pass, 94
Bridger Peak, 94
Bridger, Virginia (daughter), 62–63, 67, 68, 73, 77, 79, 90–91, 92
Bridger, William (son), 76, 77, 85, 89, 90, 92

Index

About the Author

Rosemary Palmer taught for 19 years in elementary and junior high schools. After receiving her doctorate, she became a professor at Boise State University. She has edited children's books and published professional journal articles, stories, articles for children, and a dissertation and book entitled *Children's Voices from the Trail* about children crossing the Plains. Rosemary has two grown children and two grandchildren. She lives in Idaho with her husband.

Image Credits